13 REASONS WHY
YOU SHOULD *NOT*
COMMIT SUICIDE

AND 13 REASONS WHY
YOU SHOULD LIVE

TODD FRIEL

13 Reasons Why You Should *Not* Commit Suicide

Published by:
GPM
3070 Windward Plaza, Ste. F301
Alpharetta, GA 30005

Edited by Lynn Copeland

Design and production by Genesis Group

Printed in the United States of America

ISBN 978-1-7330080-7-5

A PARABLE ABOUT YOU

Imagine you're sunbathing contentedly on a beach, but you're increasingly distracted by the shrieks of people playing in the ocean. They seem to be having far more fun in the water than you're having on the sand. You give in to temptation and go dip your toes in the water. Then your whole foot. The next thing you know, you're swimming and having a great time.

Suddenly, almost imperceptibly, an undertow pulls you into deep water. You can still hear everyone having a good time, but you aren't having fun at all. You feel alone and in over your head.

To your relief, a kindly voice from a nearby small boat says, "Take this and you will have fun again." The seemingly trustworthy stranger places a ten-pound rock in your hand and drifts away. Not only are you not having fun, this is decidedly un-fun.

The kind stranger returns and promises, "Try this and you'll be happy again." He hands you another ten-pound rock and *poof*, he's gone. As your arms and legs grow weary, the waves begin to roll over your head. You can't even hear the others having fun. You're not happy; you are scared. And exhausted.

Guess who shows up? Our kind friend hands you another stone and sincerely promises you, "Take this and you'll be safe again." You trustingly take the stone and he disappears. You feel like you are going down for the last time.

Here is my question for you: If the kindly stranger reappeared and offered you another boulder, would you take it? Of course not.

That, my friend, is a parable about you. You've been listening to voices promising you joy, fulfillment, purpose, contentment, and happiness, but those promises were lies that delivered the exact opposite.

That is what this booklet is about: the lies that have led to your dark night, and the truth that will set you free and lead you to joy. This booklet will ask you to do something radical:

- Stop believing lies.
- Start believing truth.

- Exchange your current worldview for a better set of beliefs.

You've listened to lies long enough and you're sinking. This booklet is a rope to pull you to shore, place you on dry ground, align your feet with reality, and set you on a path whose ultimate destination is *joy*. Are you ready?

HOW YOUR BRAIN WORKS

This seemingly silly exercise could be the beginning of the end of your sadness, hopelessness, and hurt. Please think this through carefully.

Imagine you are a train. In which order would you logically put your train cars, starting with the engine?

- Actions
- Emotions
- Thinking
- Believing

If you said "thinking" is the engine that pulls your other cars, then you join the majority of ancient philosophers, enlightenment thinkers, and contemporary "power of positive thinking" gurus. While it seems intuitive that thinking would drive your emotions, actions, and beliefs, the Bible puts your cars in a totally different order.

The Bible teaches that your thinking is not the engine that pulls the rest of your life along. The Bible teaches that *believing* comes first, and all of your other cars follow behind. This crucial distinction is why you are currently feeling the way you are. Let me illustrate.

Lame Illustration #1

Imagine I told you I deposited ten million dollars in your bank account. If you believed me:

- You would be ecstatic.

- Your imagination would run wild.

- You would skedaddle to your bank as fast as a shot.

Notice the order? You *believed* first, then your emotions, thinking, and actions followed. In other words, faith is the engine that drives your emotions and actions. If your life is currently off the rails, it's because your belief system is derailing you.

Permit me to take our analogy even further. Imagine you rushed to the bank to withdraw the ten million. The teller informs you that your account doesn't have ten million dollars in it. In fact, you're overdrawn. How would you feel then?

Truth would replace your joy with disappointment, anger, and a bit of desperation. You believed my lie and ended up wounded. In other words, a bad belief system has calamitous results.

My friend, that is precisely why you are feeling the way you do. The world has sold you lies and made promises it cannot keep. The world has told you:

- Believe in yourself.

- You can do anything you set your mind to.

- Money will make you happy.

- Social status and outer beauty are supremely important.

- Having more Instagram followers will make you popular.

- Get bad grades and your life is ruined.

- Get an unglamorous job and you're a failure.
- Your truth is true for you.
- You're a result of a cosmic accident.
- Life isn't precious.
- You can live any way you choose without regrets.
- Hooking up is harmless fun.
- Drinking and drugs make you feel better.
- There is no accountability.
- There is no afterlife.
- There is no God.

Those lies promised you happiness, and you believed them. You placed your trust in a godless set of values, and the world pulled the football out from under you. Now you're disappointed, angry, tired, hurting, and hopeless. The unwise thing to do is return to the same lies, hoping they will finally deliver on their promises.

After all, it was your current beliefs that brought you to your dark place. Continuing to believe the same lies cannot bring you into the light. You need a radical change. You need a new belief system. You need to stop believing lies and start believing the truth.

Jesus Christ said, "You are truly my disciples if you remain faithful to my teachings. And you will know the truth, and the truth will set you free" (John 8:31,32). Because you have not believed that truth, you are in bondage, a slave to lies.

Lame Illustration #2

What Steve Jobs is to Apple, God is to you.

Steve Jobs created Apple computers, and if you try to run an Apple with non-Apple products, you are going to experience a crash.

Similarly, God created you, and He designed you to run on His software, the Bible. If you operate with the world's understanding of reality and not His, you too are going to crash.

My friend, you need a reboot and new software. If you ever hope to live rightly and joyfully, you must exchange your false belief system for the only faith that is real and trustworthy.

God wants to replace your current software with His. When you believe Him and start importing His truth into your brain, your thinking will be gradually corrected, and your emotional monsters will progressively go away.

Jesus Christ promised, "The thief's purpose is to steal and kill and destroy. My purpose is to give them a rich and satisfying life" (John 10:10). The Bible promises you can have "God's peace, which exceeds anything we can understand" (Philippians 4:7).

If you don't have that kind of peace and joy, it is quite simple: you do not believe the One who made those promises. You may even attend church regularly, yet you have been following the world system and not the Savior.

Let God change your believing, transform your thinking, and give you joy in abundance.

If you would like to have a joy that is unspeakable, let the Bible explain thirteen reasons why you may be suicidal and the thirteen reasons why you should live. Let God change your believing, transform your thinking, and give you joy in abundance. He has done that for billions of people; He can do it for you.

REASON #1:
CONFUSION

You studied hard for an exam that will make or break your grade. Waiting for your grade to be posted is hugely stressful. Not knowing your fate can be agonizing.

Most people diagnosed with a life-threatening illness say the most excruciating time was between test taking and learning the results. Not knowing what ails you is agonizing.

Similarly, not understanding why the world is the way it is, and why we feel the way we do, is a major reason so many of us struggle to face another day. Who can blame you for being depressed when you don't know:

- What is the purpose of my existence?

- Why do I feel so rotten inside?

- Where do these black emotions come from?

- Why do I struggle while others don't seem to?

- Why don't I have hope?

- How can I make my monsters go away?

The world system cannot explain why we feel such profoundly awful emotions. Where do emotions come from? Why haven't we "evolved" beyond depression and suicidal thoughts? Why do people continue to do bad things to others? Why do we hurt one another? Why is there evil? The world offers no satisfying explanations.

The best-selling book of all time does explain why this world is the way that it is, and why you are the way you are. While this section is longer than the others, it lays the foundation for everything you need to know to lift the fog of sadness.

THE BIBLICAL SOLUTION TO CONFUSION

The Bible teaches that everything God made was absolutely perfect at creation. Adam and Eve, the first humans, lived in paradise enjoying quality time with their Maker. All was well with the world, but it didn't take long for there to be trouble in paradise.

Shortly after they were created, Adam and Eve believed the devil's lie and disobeyed God's only commandment, "Don't eat the fruit from that tree." When they rebelled against God and ate the forbidden fruit, the entire world fell from perfection and was placed under a curse (Genesis 3:17–19).

Did you catch that? Instead of believing the truth of God, Adam and Eve believed the lies of the devil. They believed Satan's promises were better, so they acted on his lies, and the consequences were disastrous. That is precisely our problem. We believe the lies of the world system (led by the devil, who Jesus called the "father of lies"), and the results are always bad.

This explains why our world is simultaneously awesome and awful. God made a beautiful planet and we humans messed it up by disobeying Him. We now live in the chapter of human history that is under a curse.

> Against its will, all creation was subjected to God's curse... For we know that all creation has been groaning as in the pains of childbirth right up to the present time. (Romans 8:20,22)

This curse explains why humans do both wonderful and awful things. This curse also explains why we feel the way we do. Not only do our bodies feel the consequences of living in an imperfect world, our brains are marred by the fall as well.

Because of sin, our thinking and emotions are not in alignment with God's thinking and emotions. We don't think or feel the way we should because our brains don't work the way they were designed to operate. You and I are victims of sin and its consequences. Thankfully, God has written another chapter of human history.

Good News

As soon as man fell for the devil's lie, God promised to send a remedy for sin. That remedy is the Son of God, Jesus Christ. He left heaven and came to earth as a man to rescue the world from the consequences of the fall.

> For God made Christ, who never sinned, to be the offering for our sin, so that we could be made right with God through Christ. (2 Corinthians 5:21)

You see, not only are we victims of sin, you and I are willing participants in sin (Romans 3:23). Sin is breaking God's moral laws. We lie, hate, steal, slander, hurt, gossip, lust, commit forbidden sexual acts, etc. God has also given us a conscience so we know right from wrong, and yet we do wrong anyway. We know we are guilty. Worse than that, we don't love God with all of our heart, soul, mind, and strength (Matthew 22:37). And let's be honest, who of us loves our neighbor as much as we love ourselves (Matthew 22:39)?

Because God is loving, good, and just, He must punish lawbreakers for their criminal behavior; that is what a just judge does. God's penalty for lawbreaking is death, followed by eternity in His prison, hell. Because we are all guilty criminals, we need someone who's innocent to rescue us from the punishment we deserve.

You and I have broken God's laws, but Jesus Christ has suffered the death penalty for us by dying on the cross, taking the punishment we deserve. Jesus was beaten, scourged, and crucified on our behalf. Then three days later He rose from the grave, defeating death. Guilty criminals can now be set free from the courtroom of God's justice because of the death and resurrection of Jesus Christ.

Consider how amazing that is. Few people would die for a good person, but Jesus died for bad people because He is that good. When you give Jesus your lengthy rap sheet, He will give you His flawless résumé.

Jesus Christ, God in the flesh, was brutally murdered at the hands of men to redeem the souls of men. God the Father bruised God the Son so justice could be satisfied and the court cases of sinners could be dismissed. By turning from your sins and trusting in Jesus, you can not only be forgiven for your crimes against God, but you will be granted eternal life with Him.

> For the wages of sin is death, but the free gift of God is eternal life through Christ Jesus our Lord. (Romans 6:23)

God promises He will one day restore this earth and make it perfect once more. Our planet is the story of a paradise created by God, paradise lost by man, and paradise regained by Jesus Christ.

One day Jesus will return to recreate His perfect paradise, but until then we live in an era of both beauty and ugliness. We experience both joys and sorrows. We feel lost because we *are* lost. People do bad things because people are bad. We suffer emotionally because our emotions are fragile and broken. Worse than that, we feel estranged from our Maker because we *are* estranged from Him.

The Big Question

Philosophers have debated the "teleological" question for millennia: What is the purpose of our existence? The world has never concocted an answer that satisfies. The Bible offers the only coherent, convincing, and consistent explanation for why things are the way they are. If you do not embrace that truth, your life will never be aligned with reality, and you will continue to feel the sting of the lies you have believed.

When you're suffering, suicide may seem attractive because it offers an end to the oppression, depression, and pain. That's a lie that's doubly tragic. If you die while your sins are unforgiven, you will not find relief from your suffering but will instead find yourself in hell for eternity. Friend, God has a much better plan for you.

God wants to adopt you into His family, forgive all your sins, progressively reorient your thinking, heal you, and give your life meaning and significance.

Why wouldn't you want to know the God who cares for you and fulfill the purpose for your existence? Why wouldn't you want to be forgiven by Jesus who loves you so much that He died for sinners like you? Why wouldn't you want to spend eternity with the most beautiful Being in the universe?

Repent (turn from your sins) and trust in Jesus Christ, and you will not only be reconciled to God and inherit everlasting life, but He will give you a new heart and put His Spirit within you to help you. God will transfer you out of darkness into light. He will move you from confusion to clarity. From lies to truth. From sadness to joy.

That is what the rest of this booklet is about, but this is your starting place: be reconciled to God.

REASON #2:
HOPELESSNESS

It has been said, "Man can live about forty days without food, about three days without water, about eight minutes without air... but only for one second without hope."[1]

Perhaps that describes you? When hope left, it took your will to live with it. Getting out of bed feels futile. School and work seem pointless. You know you should care about your future, but you don't.

Frankly, you are responding the right way to the lies the world has been peddling you. The world tells you there's no reason for your existence, and there's no life after this life. How depressing is that? If you are just worm food, then you're exactly right to feel hopeless. When this lie threatens to pull you under, the Bible gives you a reason to live.

THE BIBLICAL SOLUTION TO HOPELESSNESS

The Bible adamantly denies the lie that you are worthless worm food that will simply rot in the ground. You were created in the image of God, and He has hard-wired you to know you have a soul that will live forever (Ecclesiastes 3:11). That is why you can't shake the feeling that suicide isn't a good idea.

Knowing we will not lie in a box until we decompose but can spend eternity in heaven is the most hopeful message we will ever hear. Jesus Christ said,

> "Don't let your hearts be troubled. Trust in God, and trust also in me. There is more than enough room in my Father's home. If this were not so, would I have told you that I am going to prepare a place for you? When everything is ready, I will come and get you, so that you will always be with me where I am." (John 14:1–3)

You are not worm food. You will receive an eternal body that will live forever somewhere, either in heaven or in hell. If you have trusted in Christ, you can look forward to spending eternity with Him in a place that He is preparing just for you.

In heaven, Jesus will dry your tears (Revelation 21:4). You will have no more aches, pains, disappointments, hurt feelings, or shameful memories. It is that hope that allowed the apostle Paul to write this about his extremely crummy circumstances (shipwrecks, beatings, imprisonment, etc.):

> Yet what we suffer now is nothing compared to the glory he will reveal to us later. For all creation is waiting eagerly for that future day when God will reveal who his children really are.
>
> Against its will, all creation was subjected to God's curse. But with eager hope, the creation looks forward to the day when it will join God's children in glorious freedom from death and decay.
>
> For we know that all creation has been groaning as in the pains of childbirth right up to the present time. And we believers also groan, even though we have the Holy

Spirit within us as a foretaste of future glory, for we long for our bodies to be released from sin and suffering. We, too, wait with eager hope for the day when God will give us our full rights as his adopted children, including the new bodies he has promised us. (Romans 8:18–23)

If you are a Christian, that hope is yours too. While this life may continue to be a veil of tears, we can endure knowing not only that there is light at the end of the tunnel, but that we will live eternally with the One who is the Light of the world (John 8:12). Only Christians—those who have received God's forgiveness in Christ—have a joyful hope that is everlasting.

If you are not a Christian, you lack hope because you lack Christ. If you are a Christian lacking hope, it is because you are not remembering His great promises to you. Either way, trust Jesus. Trust Him for forgiveness. Trust Him with your future, and you will be filled with hope by the "God of hope" (Romans 15:13).

REASON #3:
PURPOSELESSNESS

The world's philosophy boils down to, "Eat, drink and be merry, for tomorrow we die." Not exactly a fulfilling way to live when you think about it. Consuming savory food and beverages is enjoyable, but it doesn't give a sense of accomplishing something significant.

Taking a trip can be a good time, but it doesn't provide a sense of purpose. Work can offer a feeling of accomplishment, but that is not the same as having purpose. Besides, even if you work hard and accumulate a bunch of nice things, when you die, someone else gets all your stuff. Or it goes in the trash. The Bible debunks this purposeless worldview and offers you a satisfying reason to keep living.

THE BIBLICAL
SOLUTION TO
PURPOSELESSNESS

Approximately 3,000 years ago, the wisest man to ever live, King Solomon, tried to find fulfillment in work, food and drink, pleasure, wealth, education, knowledge, and sex. He concluded it was all utterly worthless (Ecclesiastes 1:2). Solomon ends his gloomy treatise on godless living with a conclusion that gives meaning to *everything*:

> Here now is my final conclusion: Fear God and obey his commands, for this is everyone's duty. God will judge us for everything we do, including every secret thing, whether good or bad. (Ecclesiastes 12:13,14)

In other words, when we fear God and do everything for Him, life takes on eternal significance. A milkmaid can have joy pulling udders all day knowing she's working for the Lord and providing nourishment for God's children.

Only when we do things for God's glory do our efforts last for eternity. The world may forget you milked a million cows, but God doesn't. Even the lowliest, most mundane tasks can have eternal significance and be remembered by the King who offers rewards to His faithful servants.

No more working for the weekend. No more longing for "hump day." Every day is a day we can wake up and go to work for God Himself. Even menial tasks—such as changing diapers—are no longer trivial when they're done in service to the King.

When given the choice, seven out of ten employees said they'd prefer a better job title over a raise.[2] They believed a grandiose title had more significance than money. If you feel the same way, then here is your new title: Servant of the King. It doesn't get better than that.

REASON #4: FEAR

Fear is a correct response to something scary. Fear serves as an alarm bell that rings when you are in danger, and it can save your life. On the other hand, fear can cause you to take your life. Fear of an unknown (or bleak) future has caused many to end their lives.

Ethicists and progressives claim that physician-assisted suicide is a noble way for a person to end their life "on their own terms." Thankfully, the world lives better than their stated values. Nobody ever said, "I am so glad Kurt Cobain shot himself so he could go out on his own terms." That is because we all innately know that life is precious. There is nothing noble about intentionally ending one's life.

A godless worldview gives us permission to kill ourselves when life gets scary. Yet there is something inside each of us that screams, "I don't want to die." There is a reason for that.

THE BIBLICAL SOLUTION TO FEAR

There are countless things to fear in this world, but Jesus tells us what our greatest fear should be:

> "Don't be afraid of those who want to kill your body; they cannot touch your soul. Fear only God, who can destroy both soul and body in hell." (Matthew 10:28)

The single scariest thing in the entire world is to stand trial before God on Judgment Day, and be found guilty and cast into the flames of hell. This is why the Bible commands us over seven hundred times to fear God. God should be our number one fear, because "it is a fearful thing to fall into the hands of the living God" (Hebrews 10:31).

Great news: you do not have to fear facing a furious God on Judgment Day. If you have repented and put your trust in Jesus Christ, you will not face an angry God. You will face a God who loves you as much as He loves His Son. If you trusted in Christ, you are no longer God's enemy; you are His beloved child. Let me show you how that good news can reorient your thinking and dissipate your fears.

Picture all your earthly fears on the left side of a scale; then put the thought of an eternal hell on the right side. Then ask yourself, "How big are my temporal problems compared to my eternal problem?" That thought alone will recalibrate your thinking and help every earthly fear evaporate.

When the storms of life swirl around you and you feel like there is no break in the clouds, remember, your biggest problem has been solved. Your rotten circumstances pale in comparison to facing the wrath of God and being tossed into an eternal lake of fire.

Think of it like this: a man walks into the street and gets hit by a car. He has broken bones, internal injuries, and is bleeding profusely. Now imagine you run to help him and he says, "Please, help me get this sliver out of my finger." You would think he needs a bit of a perspective check, right?

Similarly, we need a perspective check to vanquish our fears. Our earthly problems are mere slivers compared to our God problem.

There is no need to tremble at earthly dangers when your eternal threat has been solved. Knowing Jesus spared us from the wrath that is to come will make even the most persistent fear vanish. No matter what happens in the Christian's life, we are able to sing, "It is well with my soul."

May I ask, has your eternal problem been solved? If not, Jesus stands ready to forgive you and save you from the wrath of the Just Judge of all the earth. When you repent and trust Him, your biggest problem will be solved, and your temporal and eternal fears will fade away. God doesn't desire to go to war with you. Accept His terms of surrender and He will give you peace that surpasses all understanding (Philippians 4:7).

REASON #5: GUILT

It feels like you have a relentless pursuer named Guilt. Days go by when your conscience is silent, but a sight, sound, or smell wakes your sleeping stalker and robs you of peace.

How does the world suggest we rid ourselves of the guilt we carry around like so much luggage? It says to make up for your bad deeds with good deeds. There are at least three problems with the world's guilt solution.

First, by what authority does the world claim to instruct us on non-scientific matters like morality? Science doesn't have the ability to test and determine what is moral. Without an objective source of morality (God), then all of man's morals are mere preferences.

Second, what is the math required to erase guilt? If I lie to my child, do I give $5 to the red kettle guy ringing a bell at Wal-Mart? If I have an affair, do I present my wife with one dozen roses for seven weeks?

Third, good deeds don't pay for bad deeds. Imagine a guilty criminal pleading with a judge to let him go because he was a Boy Scout who did some good deeds. It doesn't work.

Once again, the Bible can help us. If you feel guilty, it's because you *are* guilty, and the Bible offers the only solution to your guilt problem.

THE BIBLICAL SOLUTION TO GUILT

Judas Iscariot betrayed his Master, Jesus Christ. Feeling his guilt, he chose to alleviate his remorse by hanging himself (Matthew 27:3–5). Sadly for Judas, his sorrows were just beginning as he awakened to an eternity in hell (Acts 1:25). Instead of taking his own life for his sins, Judas should have trusted Jesus to take away his sins. You should too.

> "Though your sins are like scarlet, I will make them as white as snow. Though they are red like crimson, I will make them as white as wool." (Isaiah 1:18)

The solution to guilt is not good deeds or suicide, it is found in Jesus Christ who promises to cleanse you of each and every sinful deed you've ever committed. If you feel guilty and you're not yet a Christian, run to Him in repentance and faith and He will forgive you, remove your guilt, and cleanse your conscience.

If you feel guilty and you are a Christian, then you need to remember His promise that you are not guilty anymore. Stop wallowing in a pigsty that doesn't exist. Your sins have been removed from you as far as the east is from the west (Psalm 103:12). Don't feel guilty; feel forgiven. Feel joy.

REASON #6: SHAME

If every nation made a declaration that proclaimed, "Porn is a good thing," would you suddenly feel better about watching it? Nope. Society can't wave a magic wand and make shame go away. If you have done shameful things, you're likely carrying around a burden you just can't shake off.

Oprah tries to comfort with words like, "As long as you learned something, then what you did was actually a good thing." Despite her attempt to console viewers with empty clichés, we're left with memories that haunt us. The world doesn't have a solution to our shame problem, but the Bible does.

THE BIBLICAL SOLUTION TO SHAME

God loves to save bad people. He doesn't save good people because there are no good people; we have all done shameful things. Here is God's math: the more shameful you are, the more glory He receives for removing your shame.

Think of it like this. Who is kinder, the person who welcomes a celebrity into their home, or the person who takes in a homeless person? Clearly, it's the latter.

That is precisely why God loves to save the dirty, despised, weak, and broken—because it displays His great mercy and compassion in relentlessly pursuing shameful people to save.

Doing so reveals the glory of His grace and the expansive nature of His love.

Did you know that the lineage of Jesus Christ contains a former prostitute? The Bible lists the genealogy of Jesus Christ and there's a name that explodes off the page: Rahab the prostitute. That's right, Jesus had a former prostitute as an ancestor.

This woman of the evening demonstrated her faith by protecting two men from certain death (Joshua 2), and the New Testament lists her as a woman of faith (Hebrews 11:31). Because of her faith, her great, great, great, great, great, great, great grandson Jesus Christ cleansed her of her sins and gave her a "good reputation" (Hebrews 11:39).

If Jesus can forgive a prostitute and give her a good reputation, He can most certainly do the same for you. If you are a believer, lose your baggage of shame today. Give it to Jesus who bore your shame when He was shame-fully stripped naked, mocked, and hung on the cross on your behalf.

If you are an unbeliever burdened by your shame, then drop it at the foot of the cross where Jesus will forgive you and make you clean. Don't be like Judas who took his life because of guilt and shame. Join the ranks of the redeemed and you'll be listed in God's Hall of Faith thanks to Rahab's descendant Jesus Christ.

REASON #7:
EVOLUTION

Perhaps this reason for suicide surprises you, so permit me to explain why Charles Darwin's theory of origins has led to the depression of so many hurting souls.

The naturalistic worldview leads to only one conclusion: the universe is cold, impersonal, and purposeless. The only conclusions an evolutionist can draw are devastatingly depressing:

- Life is meaningless.

- You are meaningless.

- You descended from stardust.

- Your ancestors came from primordial ooze.

- Suffering has no purpose.

- Nothing you do has value.

- There is no explanation for sin and death.

- There is no ultimate justice.

- There is no afterlife to look forward to.

Is it any wonder so many people indoctrinated with this unscientific worldview are depressed? Let's consider the biblical alternative.

THE BIBLICAL SOLUTION TO EVOLUTION

Your ancestors didn't climb out of goo, go through the zoo, and eventually become you. God custom made you in your mother's womb. This is how King David put it:

> You made all the delicate, inner parts of my body and knit me together in my mother's womb. Thank you for making me so wonderfully complex! Your workmanship is marvelous—how well I know it. You watched me as I was being formed in utter seclusion, as I was woven together in the dark of the womb.

You saw me before I was born. Every day of my life was recorded in your book. Every moment was laid out before a single day had passed.

How precious are your thoughts about me, O God. They cannot be numbered! I can't even count them; they outnumber the grains of sand! And when I wake up, you are still with me! (Psalm 139:13–18)

You, my friend, are made in the image of the Maker of heaven and earth. Your life has value. Your existence has meaning. You have dignity and worth. You have a reason to live.

Before time began, God predetermined He would make you. He even has work prepared specifically for you to do (Ephesians 2:10).

Evolution is the worldview of hopelessness and death. Christianity is the worldview of life, hope, and joy.

REASON #8:
SELF-ESTEEM

The self-esteem movement is a house of cards that has collapsed on countless participants. Intended to make us feel better about ourselves, self-esteem actually leaves us feeling miserable.

How many souls have been indoctrinated with the lie that everyone is special (ironically, making nobody special)? Entire generations have been told they can accomplish anything if they simply "believe in themselves." Sadly, these people crash and burn when they step out of the self-esteem cocoon and discover they can't do everything.

There is actually a greater problem with the self-esteem lie: the Bible teaches the exact opposite. This is yet another reminder of how badly we need a reboot.

THE BIBLICAL SOLUTION TO SELF-ESTEEM

Brace yourself for this, but the Bible says two counterintuitive things that may not initially make you jump for joy:

1. Our problem is not a lack of love of ourselves. Our problem is that we love ourselves too much (Matthew 12:37–39).

2. We are not wonderful at all. The Bible goes even further by claiming that nobody is even "good" (Romans 3:10–12). We lie, cheat, steal, dishonor our parents, hate, and fail to praise our Creator the way we should. Our deeds don't shout, "You are amazing." Our sins holler, "You are totally depraved."

Hang in there, this is actually good news. Let me explain.

The self-esteem movement says you are extremely lovable; the Bible teaches that in God's eyes we are rebellious sinners who are entirely unlovable—and yet God loves us anyway. Despite who we are and what we have done, the Bible heralds, "God loves you" (John 3:16). God doesn't love us because of what we do; God loves us because of who He is.

It's a very good thing that God's love for you is not based on your lovability. You see, if God loved you because of a particular lovable feature (looks, intelligence, wit, wealth, industriousness, etc.), He would stop loving you once you fail to exhibit your wonderful attribute. Thankfully that is not how God loves.

God loves us simply because He loves us. God loves because He is love (1 John 4:8). God's love for us is transcendent and secure because His love is not based on us; it is grounded in Him. His love for you will never, ever waver, because even when you change, God never changes (Malachi 3:6).

Do you see how amazing this love is? Our fickle world and fickle friends are completely utilitarian. They love people who can provide them a benefit. A celebrity can be cheered one day and jeered the next. The world's love is fickle. God's love is not. God loves us even though we offer Him nothing.

Here are just three benefits of this kind of love:

- This love humbles us and keeps us from thinking we are better than others.

- This love gives us joy because we are loved by something far more wonderful than Facebook likes.

- All fear of man (aka peer pressure) flies out the window. Who cares what the servants think when the King says, "I love you"?

The world says, "Love yourself." The Bible says, "This is real love—not that we loved God, but that he loved us and sent his Son as a sacrifice to take away our sins" (1 John 4:10).

That truth should humble you, lift you up, and allow you to sing, "Amazing love, how can it be, that You, my God, should die for me?"

REASON #9: PORN AND HOOKING UP

Chances are extremely high you've never seen a Facebook post that read, "I don't want to brag, but I have been looking at porn every day for six years." There is just something downright shameful about porn. Despite what the world promises, porn sends men and women into a closet of shame from which they rarely escape.

Similarly, we feel unfulfilled and downright dirty after we're intimate with someone who is not our spouse. We slink away in the morning hoping the sun won't shine its spotlight on us. The world tells us to sin, then we obey and inevitably feel sin's shame. Then sin tells us to repeat the very same act that caused us shame in the first place. To quote the Wicked Witch of the West as she melted, "Oh, what a world. What a world!" Surprise—the Bible offers a better plan for sex.

THE BIBLICAL SOLUTION TO PORN AND HOOKING UP

Prepare for a radical birds-and-bees lecture from the Bible. This will forever alter your understanding of the transcendent nature of sex and lead you to something higher than drooling at pixels or "doing the nasty" with a total stranger. Let's start in the Garden.

Adam and Eve strolled in a perfect garden wearing nothing but their birthday suits. They were buck-naked and not ashamed (Genesis 2:25). It was only after eating the forbidden fruit that they realized they were naked as jaybirds. After they sinned, God clothed them to cover their sin and shame. This has many implications for us:

- Because of the fall, we don't feel comfortable when we're not covered appropriately.

- Clothing is a reminder that we are fallen, sinful beings.

- To parade around naked is to shake a fist at God and proclaim, "There is no sin, and no reason for me to cover what I am not ashamed of."

- To view others without clothing is to tell God you don't care about His rules.

When you see another naked body aside from your spouse (even on a computer screen), you're an intruder and an unwelcome observer. You are, in essence, a peeping Tom. You feel dirty after looking at porn because you've done something dirty and downright creepy.

What about hooking up, or sleeping with a boyfriend or girlfriend? Why do we feel so lousy after we do something that feels so good? There are at least two reasons.

First, when you have sex outside of marriage, you may have the other person's consent, but you don't have God's permission. God created sex and He wrote the rules of engagement. When you don't play by His rules, you'll inevitably feel guilt and shame. But there's an even more mind-blowing reason porn and hooking up leave us remorseful.

Even though sex is the most intimate and enjoyable thing a man and woman can do, it's merely a fuzzy picture of a much greater reality. The Bible tells us that the intimacy of sex is a picture of the intimate (non-sexual) relationship we will enjoy with our Savior when we are with Him in heaven (Ephesians 5).

Let me put it this way: if you think physical intimacy is amazing, wait until you get to heaven and experience spiritual intimacy with your God. Sex is the lesser pleasure that points to a greater spiritual enjoyment. Sex allows us to have a physical foretaste of the spiritual joy of heaven.

When you have sex with yourself or anyone other than your spouse, you're marring something transcendent, and you're sinning against your body (1 Corinthians 6:18). When you heed God's warning and play by His rules, you'll experience sexual intimacy on a far more profound level than any frat house experience.

Sex was designed by God to pull us up. Porn and hooking up turn us inward. God wants us to earn intimacy from our spouses. Rather than aim to "get lucky," spouses are to treat each other in such a way that they gladly give their bodies to one another. In other words, our sex drive drives us to be better people.

Porn and one-night stands enable us to live only for self. They do not make us nobler, they make us more selfish. When you watch porn or hook up, you have no reason to become the person someone would happily give himself or herself to.

If you are depressed and you're watching porn or hooking up, there is a connection. Let God rewire your thinking so you can enjoy sex the way He has prescribed. Determine to be done with lesser things once and for all.

Should you happen to think that God cannot forgive your past sexual indiscretions (or even perversions), let me lovingly tell you as emphatically as possible: *you are wrong!* God is more than willing to wash you clean, and in a sense, make you pure again. Don't delay, repent and trust Jesus today, and He will make you white as snow.

REASON #10: ABORTION

Let's be honest, there are very few women (and men) who don't feel a crushing sense of grief, guilt, and loss after aborting their baby. Here are a few of the world's lies designed to justify ending the life of an unborn child:

"It's just a small blob of tissue." While that is certainly true, it's not okay for a basketball player to kill a jockey just because he's shorter. Hurting someone small and helpless is the behavior of bullies.

"It isn't fully developed." Neither are children, but we all mourn when we hear about grade school shootings. Level of development is irrelevant to the value of a human life.

"It's the woman's body." Since when does location make someone more or less human? Traveling eight inches down a birth canal doesn't magically transform a blob into a baby. A human's environment doesn't give us the right to kill it.

"It depends on the mother to survive. It's a parasite." Yep, and two-year-olds depend on

their mothers to survive too. But that doesn't give us the right to kill toddlers.

"It's the product of rape or incest." While those acts are particularly evil, the blob is still a baby regardless of how it was conceived. Why kill an innocent baby when we should be punishing the criminal?

Cruelly, the world tells you to celebrate your abortion. But we know intuitively that a party is not the right response to such a wrong act. The Bible offers a much better alternative for our sinful guilt and shame.

THE BIBLICAL SOLUTION TO ABORTION

Is there any hope for you if you have participated in an abortion? Absolutely. There is no sin too big for the amazing grace of Jesus.

You don't need to feel guilt and shame any more. Jesus promises to forgive even the most wicked sins if the sinner will come to Him in genuine repentance and faith. Once you have received His forgiveness, there is no more guilt and no more shame.

You don't have to be a second-class Christian because of your past. Those who've had abortions can be forever adopted into God's family and are no less forgiven than any of His children. Grace is that big. God is that good.

Lose your guilt and shame; repent of *all* your sins and trust in Jesus. Then spend the rest of your days filled with joy because you have been forgiven of each and every sin, including the sin of abortion. And when God takes you home, you will see your precious baby in heaven.

REASON #11:
ABANDONMENT
AND ABUSE

If you were abandoned as a child, you know there's no pain like family pain. Daycare, divorce, and distracted parents are hurts felt deeper than perhaps any other wound inflicted on a child.

If your parents abandoned you (even if they were still living in the house), you ache. I am terribly sorry. There is healing available to you.

47

Physical, sexual, emotional, and spiritual abuse are painful in more ways than one. Even though the bruises and broken bones heal, emotional scars remain. If you are the victim of abuse, let me again say how sorry I am. Please make sure you're in a safe place before you continue reading.

Abuse and abandonment share a similar component: they are both encouraged by a lie from the world. The world tells us to love ourselves above all things and seek personal happiness before the happiness of others. Is it any wonder so many of us have been abandoned or abused by people who love themselves more than they love us?

THE BIBLICAL SOLUTION TO ABANDONMENT AND ABUSE

The Bible tells us to regard others as more important than ourselves (Philippians 2:3) and to love our neighbors, not hurt them (Mark 12:31). The Bible tells us to defend the vulnerable, not abuse them (Psalm

82:3,4). Scripture is clear that God loves marriage and hates divorce (Malachi 2:16) and that God wants mommies and daddies to stay together for life (Mark 10:7–9).

Whenever we alter God's recipe for living, as given in the Bible, pain is inevitable. Children are called a precious gift from God; abusing them is never God's design. Placing our children in the care of strangers is not God's design. Divorce is not God's desire. Parents who pay little attention to a child isn't God's intention for family.

If you have been abandoned, there is hope and healing for you. Jesus Christ promises to never leave you, forsake you, or hurt you (Hebrews 13:5). Your pain can be soothed, your anger calmed, and your tears turned into laughter. Healing is not a mere possibility for Christians who have been wounded; it is a wonderful reality.

If you were abused, God was not sleeping, distant, or unaware. Rest assured, God saw the evil inflicted on you and tolerated it, but He has not forgotten it. He recorded those events in a book (Revelation 20:12) and He will settle the score with those who have committed wicked deeds against His image bearers.

Even if the police don't deal with your abuser, God most certainly will. And God's justice is far more exacting than any earthly penal system. All abusers will pay the penalty for their sins, or Jesus will have paid it for them if they turn to Him in repentance. Either way, justice will be served.

This little booklet cannot begin to unpack all the ways that God will work to heal you. If you would like to learn how God heals emotional wounds, please visit Rickthomas.net and search for: abuse, anger, unforgiveness. You will see that God has the means to make you whole and even return your joy.

REASON #12: SOCIAL MEDIA

You'd be hard-pressed to find a study on suicide that didn't include the effects of social media. The idealized images we see on the Internet leave an indelible mark. Social media tells you that you're not as pretty, handsome, happy, thin, and amazing as everyone else.

The world's response to your disappointment is to peddle you more beauty products, weight-loss programs, fancy clothes, facelifts, fitness plans, and empty mantras. Hardly a recipe for joy.

THE BIBLICAL SOLUTION TO SOCIAL MEDIA

It's difficult to find anyone today who doesn't suffer from body-image issues. But of thousands of individuals mentioned in the Bible, only a handful are described as beautiful or handsome. Why is this?

> The LORD doesn't see things the way you see them. People judge by outward appearance, but the LORD looks at the heart. (1 Samuel 16:7)

God isn't enthralled with physical beauty; He is interested in spiritual beauty. He's not concerned with outward appearances; He is concerned with inner character. God isn't wowed by good looks; God is pleased when we look and behave like Jesus Christ…who the Bible says wasn't an outwardly good-looking man (Isaiah 53:2).

The world and your mirror may tell you that you aren't a supermodel, but God tells you that you're fully pleasing to Him if you are His child. If you have been adopted into His family, there is nothing you can do to be more accepted and loved by God than you already are. Because of that great news, we strive not for outer beauty, but for the things that are precious to God.

> Don't be concerned about the outward beauty of fancy hairstyles, expensive jewelry, or beautiful clothes. You should clothe yourselves instead with the beauty that comes from within, the unfading beauty of a gentle and quiet spirit, which is so precious to God. (1 Peter 3:3,4)

If you are a Christian, the Lord will actually "rejoice over you with joyful songs" (Zephaniah 3:17). Who cares what the world thinks when the Lord of all creation sings, "I love you"? If you want to look in the mirror and judge yourself, then judge yourself accepted, adopted, and loved.

Lifestyle Disappointment

According to the Internet, everyone is living the high life, which is supposedly the best life to live. That is a double lie.

1. Nobody lives a pain-free and trouble-free life. Nobody.

2. Big homes, exotic vacations, and lavish life-styles are *not* the significant things of life.

Would you rather live a life being chased by the paparazzi, or would you rather be forgiven, adopted, and granted everlasting life by the Creator of the universe?

Besides, when Jesus returns, He is going to burn up all this stuff and make a new heaven and a new earth. While creature comforts are nice, they're going to be kindling for the biggest bonfire the world has ever seen when paradise is recreated.

Additionally, we're going to live in a better place than any mansion ever built. We get to live in a place that Jesus Himself is preparing for us (John 14:2,3).

Who cares about the lesser things when we have the greatest thing, God Himself? Let the world have momentary pleasures and chase its tail. Let the world seek vain things; God's promises to His children are infinitely greater:

> You will show me the way of life, granting me the joy of your presence and the pleasures of living with you forever. (Psalm 16:11)

Worldly things are mere idols, and idols always break the hearts of their worshipers. Don't be deceived and settle for trinkets that never satisfy. Seek the things that are transcendent and eternal. Seek the things that will bring you joy.

REASON #13: LONELINESS

Mark Zuckerberg promises that Facebook is the only community anyone needs. That is another lie. You can have hundreds of online "friends," get thousands of likes, and still feel totally alone.

Not only can Mr. Zuckerberg not remove our loneliness, he can't even explain why humans feel lonely in the first place. The Bible has an explanation and better promises than Mr. Zuckerberg offers.

THE BIBLICAL SOLUTION TO LONELINESS

The Bible explains that we feel blue when we don't participate in genuine relationships, because we were made to live in relationship with other people—just like our Creator.

God is one God who exists in three Persons: Father, Son, and Holy Spirit. In other words, God lives in community. As God's image bearers, we resemble and reflect Him in many ways. Humans are made to live in community because the One who made us lives in community. When we don't cultivate relationships, we are not living the way we were designed to live; hence, we experience loneliness.

Thankfully, God has provided three communities for us to live in that will keep us from ever feeling lonely again:

Community one: God. If you are a Christian, you are in a personal relationship with the Creator of heaven and earth. Even when you're by yourself, you are never alone. He is an ever-present help even in times of trouble (Psalm 46:1).

If you are a Christian, you are in a personal relationship with the Creator of heaven and earth.

Community two: the local church. As individuals who have been adopted into God's family, Christians get to live with our fellow adopted brothers and sisters in the context of a local church. Can it be annoying? Yes. But it can also be the sweetest place on earth.

Community three: the communion of saints, that is, everyone who has ever been saved. When you repent and place your faith in Jesus, you are instantly adopted into a family of billions. You share a bond and unity with every Christian who is alive or in heaven. The new believer instantly has more "friends" than Facebook can ever provide.

Let me give you a sneak peek into your future if you are in the family of God. This is the apostle John's revelation of heaven:

> After this I saw a vast crowd, too great to count, from every nation and tribe and people and language, standing in front of the throne and before the Lamb. They were clothed in white robes and held palm branches in their hands. And they were shouting with a great roar, "Salvation comes from our God who sits on the throne and from the Lamb!"...
>
> "They will never again be hungry or thirsty; they will never be scorched by the heat of the sun. For the Lamb on the throne will be their Shepherd. He will lead them to springs of life-giving water. And God will wipe every tear from their eyes." (Revelation 7:9,10,16,17)

If you have repented and trusted in Jesus Christ, you will be in that amazing scene with your brothers and sisters from all over the globe. Until then, you can live in a real community with people who love you, serve you, and sacrifice for you in a local church.

This world can be cold and cruel, but in God's family you never have to be lonely again. Friends may abandon you, but the Lord and His people will never leave you nor forsake you (Hebrews 13:5).

LET THE REBOOT BEGIN

Have you seen it? Have you seen how a godless worldview tells lie after lie that leads to futility? Have you seen how God's Word is the truth you need to live a life that makes sense?

My friend, the world has been lying to you for long enough. Today is the day to start believing the truth.

Suicide isn't your only option; in fact, it's your worst option.

Don't take your life. Instead, surrender your life to Jesus, the Lord of Life, and He will reveal more and more truth to you, fix your thinking, and heal your broken heart. Best of all, He will take you to be with Him in heaven when He decides to call you home.

Be done with the lies of the world and be reconciled to the God of truth. Then join a Bible-based church and experience deep, profound, and real relationships, instead of shallow, fickle social media experiences that leave us feeling so lonely.

- Will your troubles disappear? Not necessarily.

- Will you never feel blue again? Not necessarily.

- Will you immediately feel perfect? Not necessarily.

God will patiently work with you as you work with Him to change your thinking, emotions, and actions. This will require effort from you. Healing is not a passive activity. You have laid down a lot of tapes in your mind; it will take a long time to erase and replace them.

As a Christian, you will be asked by God to stop doing a lot of things (looking at porn, hooking up, believing lies). He is also going to ask you to do a lot of things (read your Bible, join a church and serve, fill your brain with truth). As you do those things, with His help, God will progressively heal you as He reforms you and inevitably makes you look more and more like His amazing Son.

God offers you a genuine fresh start today. The God who created the world and sent His Son to rescue sinners can most certainly rescue you. God loves you and cares about your tears.

Jesus promised that you can have life abundantly, and He never lies. You can have forgiveness, joy, and hope. You can have it starting right now.

What are you waiting for?

> I pray that God, the source of hope, will fill you completely with joy and peace because you trust in him. Then you will overflow with confident hope through the power of the Holy Spirit. (Romans 15:13)

MORE HELP

The Bible says that we all need help. You do *not* need to feel embarrassed if you need help too. You are not odd, and Christians will not treat you as if you are.

Help Center #1: Church

You can find a Bible-based church and people who care about you here: founders.org/church-search.

Find the church closest to you, call them to introduce yourself, and ask for a meeting with the pastor. Meet with him and share where you are regarding your beliefs, thoughts, and emotions. There is nothing you can say that will shock him. Nothing. Your secrets and your pain are safe with him. Pastors are trustworthy men who would *love* to help you.

If you think your life is too messed up to join a bunch of goody two-shoes people, then let me assure you, no matter how much we dress up on Sunday morning, we all feel the effects of our sin. You are not alone; you are among friends in the church.

Help Center #2: A Counselor

If you would like a biblical counselor to walk alongside you and work through your struggles, please visit: Christiancounseling.com/network/find-a-counselor.

You may find a counselor near you, but if you don't, you can receive counseling long distance. Please interview as many counselors as you need to until you find one you feel comfortable with.

What About Psychiatry and Medication?

Christianity doesn't teach that no one will ever need psychotropic medication. But in general medication is needed by a small percentage of the people who receive those prescriptions. If you're taking medication for depression, do not go off your meds until you spend time with your doctor *and* your pastor or biblical counselor. While you may need these medications, you may not. Proceed slowly.

If you are currently being counseled by someone who doesn't use the Bible as the sole source of information for spiritual maladies like depression and suicidal thoughts, please find a biblical counselor who does. A secular therapist cannot get to the root of your problems and offer you the hope that is found only in the God of all hope. .

SCRATCHING THE SURFACE

This booklet barely scratches the surface of the truths of the Christian faith. This information is intended only to point you in the right direction: to the Savior who can cleanse you of sin, give you eternal life, and transform you into a new person. Then, in the context of the local church, you will experience ongoing change for the rest of your life.

Thank you for the privilege of your company. I look forward to meeting you someday in church, or in heaven. Permit me to close with this quote from a seventeenth-century preacher named Thomas Brooks.

> There is in a crucified Jesus—something proportionate to all the difficulties, needs, trials, and desires of His poor people. Jesus is...
> *bread* to nourish them,
> a *garment* to cover and adorn them,

a *physician* to heal them,
a *counselor* to advise them,
a *captain* to defend them,
a *prince* to rule them,
a *prophet* to teach them,
a *priest* to atone for their sin,
a *husband* to protect them,
a *father* to provide for them,
a *brother* to relieve them,
a *foundation* to support them,
a *head* to guide them,
a *treasure* to enrich them,
a *sun* to enlighten them, and
a *fountain* to cleanse them!

What more can any Christian desire...
to *satisfy* him and *save* him,
to make him *holy* and *happy*,
both in time and in eternity![3]

NOTES

1. Famous Quotes & Authors <tinyurl.com/yyjfz3ve>.
2. John Ezard, "Seven out of 10 office staff prefer grander job title to pay rise," *The Guardian*, April 18, 2000 <tinyurl.com/y6576lg8>.
3. Thomas Brooks, "The Golden Key to Open Hidden Treasures" Grace Gems, <tinyurl.com/yyk4ck75>.